Ballad of Jamie Allan

WITHDRAWN

LIBRARY ST. MARY'S COLLEGE

COPYRIGHT © 2007 BY TOM PICKARD

ALL RIGHTS RESERVED

FOR PERMISSION, REQUIRED TO REPRINT OR

BROADCAST MORE THAN SEVERAL LINES, WRITE TO:

FLOOD EDITIONS, POST OFFICE BOX 3865

CHICAGO, ILLINOIS 60654-0865

WWW.FLOODEDITIONS.COM

ISBN 978-0-9787467-4-2

DESIGN AND COMPOSITION BY QUEMADURA

COVER AND INTERIOR ILLUSTRATIONS:

WOOD ENGRAVINGS BY THOMAS BEWICK (1753–1828)

THIS BOOK WAS MADE POSSIBLE IN PART

THROUGH A GRANT FROM THE ILLINOIS ARTS COUNCIL

PRINTED ON ACID-FREE, RECYCLED PAPER

IN THE UNITED STATES OF AMERICA

FIRST EDITION

Contents

THE CHARM 1

PETER KEMP OF CAVILL, HIS INFORMATION 2

ROBT. ALLAN, HIS INFORMATION 3

DURHAM LOCKUP 4

GENERAL HUE AND CRY 5

MATTHEW ROBINSON, HIS INFORMATION 6

HEY UP AND AWAY 7

JAMES ALLAN, HIS INFORMATION 12

MARCH HORSES 13

JOHN BELL, HIS INFORMATION 14

ANNIE BENNETT, HER INFORMATION 15

NEWCASTLE COURANT 17

BLACK ACT 19

DURHAM LOCKUP 21

AWAY BOYS AWAY 22

DURHAM LOCKUP 24

RALPH SOULSBY ESQ., JUSTICE OF
   THE PEACE, HIS INFORMATION 25

DURHAM LOCKUP: THE GREAT OBJECT 27

FAST FUCKING LEGS 28

NEWCASTLE COURANT 41

JOIN THE ARMY 42

WAR OFFICE 45

WAR OFFICE 46

FETCH THE MAN AWAY 47

DURHAM LOCKUP: DESERTER 48

NELL CLARK 49

DURHAM LOCKUP 53

THOMAS RIDLEY, HIS INFORMATION 54

JOHN CLARK, HIS INFORMATION 58

JOHN CLARK, HIS INFORMATION 65

ROBERT LOWRY, HIS INFORMATION 69

WALTER SCOTT, HIS INFORMATION 71

A LOW SKY 73

THE RIVER IS DARK 74

BALLAD OF PRECIPITATION 76

HAWTHORN 77

BALLAD OF JAMIE ALLAN 79

DURHAM LOCKUP 82

NEWCASTLE COURANT 83

"CLOUDS DRAG SHADOWS

   ACROSS CONTOURS" 84

AFTERWORD 89

SELECTED RESOURCES 95

ACKNOWLEDGEMENTS 99

*The memory of bandits has been preserved
by their association with particular places.*

ERIC HOBSBAWM, *Bandits*

*It was as if the Border people had dreamed Gregorio Cortez before
producing him, and had sung his life and his deeds before he was born.*

AMÉRICO PAREDES, *'With His Pistol
in His Hand': A Border Ballad and Its Hero*

*Against the law, against the rich, the powerful, the magistrates,
the constabulary or the watch, against taxes and their collectors,
he appeared to have waged a struggle with which one all too easily
identified. The proclamation of these crimes blew up to epic propor-
tions the tiny struggle that passed unperceived in everyday life.*

MICHEL FOUCAULT, *Discipline and
Punish: The Birth of the Prison*

Redistribution of wealth.

WACHOWSKI BROTHERS, *Bound*

*Besides, I have a Prison Scene, which the Ladies
always reckon charmingly pathetick.*

JOHN GAY, *The Beggar's Opera*

Ballad of Jamie Allan

THE CHARM

you who make music
and music makes
whose fingers fly
make of air a song
your breath be steady
and the tune be long

PETER KEMP OF CAVILL, HIS INFORMATION

13TH JANUARY 1694

.about Christmas last hee had a ten
shillinge and piece of goold
taken out of his Chest
and that within this four or five days
hee had ten in goold and fortie shillings in monie
taken outt of his chambere
and that hee found his Goold and silver
with Robt Allan.

ROBT. ALLAN, HIS INFORMATION

13TH JANUARY 1694

martinmass last hee was looking for some of his Linnin
in Petter Kemps chest
hee found a tenn shillings pece of goold
and that yesterday morn being the twelfth
hee looking for kecks
under Petter Kemps bed
found a purse with monie in itt butt
how much there was
hee knew nott.

DURHAM LOCKUP

13TH NOVEMBER 1810

Beneath a bridge that spans the river
a low wind invades his cell
and withers the thin afternoon light.
Jamie Allan is seventy-seven years old and dying.
The wind smells of the Wear, sprays rain on the wall
and growls
with an insistent swither.
He pulls a ragged blanket close,
leaving an ear exposed to the crack.
Chaff flatters the rats.

GENERAL HUE AND CRY

NEWCASTLE COURANT, 26TH MARCH 1803

Stolen, between the 24th–25th of the instant March, out of the Stable, a bay Horse, 6 years old, with a white Face, slack in the Shoulder, and uncommon high on the Back, the far hind Leg white shorn on each Buttock, and about Fifteen Hands high; Whoever will bring him to Matthew Robinson, at the Old Chapel, Gateshead, The Owner, shall be handsomely rewarded for their trouble.

MATTHEW ROBINSON, HIS INFORMATION

16TH MAY 1803

Durham to wit}

The Informant upon his oath saith that between the hours of ten in the evening of Thursday the twenty fourth day of March last and seven in the following morning the stable of the informant was feloniously broken and entered into, and a Bay Gelding the property of this informant feloniously stolen taken and carried away. And this informant further saith, on the same night he saw two persons with a child proceeding thereupon, one of whom he then knew to be James Allan: that this informant demanding what such person was doing there was answered by the said Allan that they had lost their way and wanted to be at Gateshead Fell to which this informant replied do you want the High or Low fell? but receiving no answer proceeded homeward.

HEY UP AND AWAY

The informant further saith
on the twenty-fourth of March
returning to his dwelling house
when it was getting dark
he saw two persons and a child
proceeding thereupon.
The informant then demanded
the travellers be gone.

Hey up! Hey up! Hey up and away!

I told him we were lost
and wanting Gateshead Fell.
Do you want the high or low?
Matthew Robinson did yell,
both are haunts of rogues
and villains like yasels.
Young Annie turned a look
that scudded him to hell.

Matthew slammed the gate
he shut it in wa faces,

the wind blew sleet all neet
wor skran was only traces.
The gate was shut a bolt was drawn
he sent us on our way
then fell into his feather bed
and slept there warm till day.

Hey up! Hey up! Hey up and away!

When he got up his horse was gone
and so was Jamie Allan.
The sun was up the hail had stopped
Matthew Robinson got gannin.
He raised a hue he raised a cry
a call out for his nag
and a special word he put about
to catch a bag of rags.

He asked the turnpike captain,
did you see him come this way?
When he came past was he upon
my strong and sturdy bay?
He's six years old, high in the back
and in the shoulder slack—

did you see him come this way
and did you let him pass?

I saw your gipsy piper
and he was riding high
saddled on your gelding
and laughing in your eye.
He took the border road,
a cold wind at his tail.
The devil rode behind him
and they burnt a northern trail.

Hey up! Hey up! The devil on his tail!

Matthew crossed the border,
he took the quiet roads
looking for a tinker—
a man of no abode.
Then creeping down Thief Sike
and owa Liddel Watta
he heard the sound of pipes
that whittled into laughter.

He rode up Lady Knowe
and down to Hartsgarth Flow,

he trotted through the Reagill Boggs
still deep in winter snow.
He thought he caught a sight
down on the Windy Slack
but when he reached the Starcleugh Edge
he was way off track.

He then went up to Wether Law
onto the Lightning Hill
and thought he caught a whiff
along the Cumcleugh Gill.
He heard I was at Langburnshiel
and with the constable gave chase;
they rode hard and they rode long
but could not keep apace.

When they found me I was sleeping
in a bed of heather;
they put a gun against my face
and tied me to a tether.
You are the gypsy piper
and you were riding high
saddled on my gelding
and laughing in my eye.

I am the gypsy piper
and still I'm riding high
saddled on your gelding
and laughing in your eye.
You howked me at the border,
cold winds tell this tale.
The devil rides beside you
and he drinks the hangman's ale.

JAMES ALLAN, HIS INFORMATION

16TH MAY 1803

Taken in the city of Durham before me Richard Prosser, Doctor of Divinity and William Masefield clerk to his Majesty's Justice of The Peace for the County of Durham the sixteenth day of May.

Durham to wit} The Examination of James Allan of North Shields in the County of Northumberland the Piper Who ~~saith that~~ on being charged on the oath of Matthew Robinson of Gateshead in the county of Durham banksman with having on the night of Thursday the twenty fifth day of March last in the year of our Lord One thousand Eight hundred and three stolen taken and carried away a Bay Gelding the property of the said Matthew Robinson—and being called on to give an account of how he came by the possession of the said Bay Gelding, the said James Allan saith that he bought the said Bay Gelding on a Saturday the latter end of March last (he thinks the 26th) on the road as he was going to, and on the South side, Alnwick in Northumberland and therefore he denies the charge of having stolen the said Bay Gelding from the said Matthew Robinson.

MARCH HORSES

wind tunnels
a hill's furrow

where crows hang and skate

two black blades
slicing air and less

than a feather
between them

JOHN BELL,
HIS INFORMATION

7TH MARCH 1776

On Monday night John Bell's stables were screwed
and his black mare went missing.

On Tuesday morning, early, Richard Thompson
found a chestnut Galloway gelding, a black mare, a saddle
and a bridle missing from his stables.

Thomas Trumble looking for his Shetland ponies and Galloways
met John Bell—who said it's market day at Edinburgh
they'll be selt there—and rode north together.

They gave out exact descriptions of their animals
and by eight o'clock that night heard of a sighting
on the Glasgow Road at sunrise.

But they lost track, gave up the chase and turned south
where they met the black mare 'with Jamie Allan on its back'
and his brother Robert riding the other.

ANNIE BENNETT,
HER INFORMATION

The sound of deep waters sang in my sleep
so I followed the stream to search for a thief.
I followed a dark stream that ran underground;
by the sound of deep waters my lover was found.

The sound of fast water running like blood
played me a music that I understood.
When I heard the dark music I thought I would drown;
by the sound of deep waters my lover was found.

Through a pool of dark waters run fresh from the fell
ran the fast-running waters to a deep-sounding well.
By the sound of dark laughter and thyme-covered ground,
by the fast-running waters my lover was found.

I went to the castle in old Durham town
and asked at the gatehouse would they bring him down.
The jailor all smiles said, 'Step dear within,
hear your old gypsy piper play till he swings.

'He's been trouble and grief from his damn birth,
deserter and thief and many things worse,
but we have your traveller and here he will stay
chained up in heavy iron till his 'sizes day.'

And who will you get to play all day and neet
for the farm lads and lasses that bring in the wheat?
And what can we swallow, his babby and me,
if he rots, a ripe fruit on an orchard tree?

'You can plead to the judge and bring him a note
to loosen the knot drawn close to his throat,
but when he refuses what jigging there'll be
to the tune of the wind in the hanging tree.'

NEWCASTLE COURANT

6TH AUGUST 1803

The prisoners return grateful thanks to his Grace the Duke of Northumberland for his benevolent donation of five guineas. Yesterday his Grace and family passed through Newcastle on their way to Alnwick Castle.—Every honest Northumbrian will no doubt be proud, at this moment of crisis, to be again honoured, after so long an absence, with his Grace's presence.— He looked remarkably well. We hear from Alnwick, that on Friday the 5th instant the Duke and Duchess, Earl Percy, and the young Lady Percies, arrived at the castle there, the noble mansion of that illustrious family. The Duke's ill state of health not having permitted him to visit Northumberland for some years past, his Grace was, on the above occasion, ushered into the county with every demonstration of joy and welcome, highly expressive of the popularity in which the noble Duke is justly held by all ranks, as well in respect of his public as his private character. On the Duke's approach towards Alnwick, his numerous tenants in that neighbourhood, to the amount of several hundreds, came forward to Felton, to meet his Grace and his amiable family, and attend them to their Castle. Notwithstanding his Grace's earnest solicitations to the contrary, the people insisted upon taking his horses out of his carriage and drawing it through the town of Alnwick to the Castle, amidst repeated cheers, ringing of bells, firing of cannon, &c. At the Durham Assizes, James Allan, of North Shields, the famous piper, aged 77, for stealing a horse out of the stables of Matthew Robinson, of Gateshead, was found guilty, DEATH.

BLACK ACT

DURHAM ASSIZES, AUGUST 1803

When the judges came to clean out their prison
the gentry of Durham laid on fine provision;
they drank to their health and spoke to their wealth
and without taking breath sang a sentence of death.

Jamie Allan before them, at the age of seventy,
took a horse from Gateshead, where they had plenty,
and rode it to Scotland to sell it for skran
followed by the posse who knew where he would gan.

The judge put on his best black act his flowing robes so lang.
The judge put on his best black act and told them he will hang.
The judge put on his best black act his black cap and his cloak.
Here's a rope to stroke his throat, his windpipe till he chokes.

I met an honest man, my lord, his name was never told,
he sold the creature to me on the Alnwick Road,
then later when I rode it, my legs are old and tired,
a posse came along with the constable that fired.
I thought that they were robbers with intent to steal

so rode the creature hard to hide at Langburnshiel.
The clerk stood up and rang a heavy bell.
My Lord will now address you, will you greet the Earl of Hell.

The judge put on his best black act his flowing robes so lang.
The judge put on his best black act and told him he must hang.
The judge put on his best black act, his black cap and his cloak.
Here's a rope to stroke your throat, your windpipe till you choke.

The judge took up his flowing gown.
Fetch up the felon and tek him down,
the piper's pipes will stop the ringing
when the piper and the rope are swinging.
A rough hemp rope is fine enough for gypsies and their ilk,
or pay to hang like a gentleman and dangle in silk.
The judge stood up and Jamie Allan fell.
My Lord went to his chambers and the piper to his cell.

DURHAM LOCKUP

13TH NOVEMBER 1810

The wind comes in waves that roll
and shift and taste of salt.
They showed clemency and my sentence was cut
to transportation.

A few days after Annie Bennett declined my offer
I asked her to collect a parcel
from the captain of a ship moored at North Shields.
And while he entertained her in his cabin
the crew slipped the line
and the boat drifted on the tide.

As it passed the bar she rushed on deck and found me
so I introduced 'my wife' to the crew.
She flew into a rage worse than any storm I've known.
Then she was becalmed and we married on the waters.
She is my niece.

AWAY BOYS AWAY

I asked my love to be my bride
and come with me on the swelling tide
to sail the seas and the oceans wide
away boys away

I thought my love my love would bless
when I brought my love a crimson dress
but the crimson dress did not impress
away boys away

I said I would not be his bride
so he stole me away on the red'ning tide
and sailed me out to the ocean wide
away boys away

a storm blew up and we changed course
she ripped and tossed a raging horse
she raged and threatened my demise
my love my love she did despise

I said I would not be his bride
then fell becalmed on the swelling tide
the music my wild piper plays
drives the storm and stills the waves

away boys away

DURHAM LOCKUP

13TH NOVEMBER 1810

The wind's in a hurry tonight. It hassles the frame
but never the lock. It lifts the slates but never the roof.
It jabs the window like a bailiff. Or shoulders the door
like redcoats hunting deserters.

There was another petition against the transportation,
pleading age, ill health and probable death at sea.
There have been many petitions,
many gentlemen have interceded for my life.

RALPH SOULSBY ESQ., JUSTICE OF THE PEACE, HIS INFORMATION

15TH NOVEMBER 1760

My Lord on Thursday last I met with a Sergeant and Drummer belonging to Mr Sloho, Ensign of the first division of Marines now recruiting at Hexham, who had that instant apprehended a Deserter whose name is James Allan, late of Rothbury in this County, and who tell me he deserted from his Grace the Duke of Richmond's Regiment but knows not his Captain's name. He was much in liquor and through the assistance of an idle fellow then with him attempted an escape. I have issued my warrant to apprehend the person that assisted and shall publicly punish him by whipping or otherwise, as your Lordship will order. Allan received a most violent cut on his wrist from the drummer's sword. I immediately ordered a Surgeon to attend him who tells me he will have the use of his hand. I have presumed to confine him in a Prison at Hexham until I am honoured with your Lordship's further direction. I am with great respect your Lordship's most obedient humble servant.

P.S. However unwilling to excuse an offence such as this kind I humbly beg your Lordship will allow the presumption I now take of begging the poor man's life as he really is a great object.

DURHAM LOCKUP: THE GREAT OBJECT

13TH NOVEMBER 1810

It had to be a drummer!
I still can't bend some fingers.
I told him, you've ruined the best pipe hand in England.

I could still play but
it stopped my lucrative join-ups and jump-outs.
The army paid five guineas bounty and I enlisted
with two recruiting parties on the same day, once.
It was quick money if you had a slow face
and fast fucking legs.

FAST FUCKING LEGS

1

On the trot from a Liverpool recruiting party,
who had his pipes,
he told the landlady of The Plough
he'd been walking all night
and would have to sleep till he woke,
then kept low until dark
when he took to the road again
travelling through the night
until he came to a barn about dawn
where he hid until dusk
eating boiled eggs and bread
he'd brought from The Plough.

Passing through Darlington he met a group
of Cumberland tinkers who threw a party
for two days and nights.
When all but a hangover and a shilling
of the sign-up money was left
he headed North
to collect his pipes.

But after so long gone
he didn't want to turn up skint.

Will you have a drink with the army?
a recruiting sergeant at Durham asked
and tickled his trout into signing—on condition, he accepted,
the bounty money would be paid up front
so that his new recruit could
'pay a few debts and meet an obligation, y'kna.'

Allan was thinking
how he could had away with himself
and the money
but he was placed in a billet
with a bayonet-eyed corporal
who liked a bevy.
And it was Jamie's treat
till he keeled over and the piper—
in need of clean linen—took the soldier's shirt
and a stroll after asking
an ostler the road to Chester-le-Street.

Once out of sight he turned back
and holed up in a travelling cooper's gaff
where he 'dressed his hair and altered his dress'

and left
after three days because there was a posse out
for the cooper.
Allan took off to the toon to grab a good suit
—cos you don't get the gigs if you don't got the look.

2

Newcastle Courant, SATURDAY, 4TH OCTOBER 1760

Deserted from the 56th Regiment of Foot, commanded by Major-general Lord Charles Manners; he inlisted in the name of James Allan with Captain Grey, of Kinsley, some years past, and after that, at the Battle of St Cass, defected to the French; he is a Piper, and comes from near Rothbury, five feet, eight and one quarter inches high, straight limb'd, and well made, a round large Head, flat Face, dark brown Hair under his Wig, which is a light coloured clipt one; had on, when he deserted, a Dark Drab Coat, with Buttons of the same Colour, brown linen Waistcoat, and Buttons of the same, white Worsted Shag Breeches, and grey ribb'd Stockings; Enlisted the 17th of September 1760, at the City of Durham, and deserted from Newcastle on the 19th of the same Month. Whoever secures the above Deserter in any of his Majesties Gaols in Great Britain, and gives notice to the Commanding Officer of the said Regiment, shall receive Twenty Shillings reward over and above what is allowed by Act of Parliament.

3

Two greet grenadiers grabbed him on Bottle Bank
and marched him to the guard-house
because a deserter was posted and he fit the bill.
An officer sent to Durham for the recruiting sergeant
to I.D. the suspect.

Allan 'requested to be shewn backwards'
and the officer ordered a private to go with him
and stand guard outside the privy.
After a time he called out without reply
and when he opened the door
Jamie Allan was gone.

The private was arrested for collusion
until a sergeant, following the scent, put him right.

Allan crawled through the sewers
until he found an exit at Gallowgate
and after hiding in furze

escaped across the town moor—sometimes,
at a leeward distance, joining the search for himself.

His first thought was yem,
but he stunk of shite so went to Morpeth
and stayed with a member of the 'Faa gang'
who cleaned him up and out of sight.
The town's coops were plucked for a feast
where he peddled his tales.

All next day he hid until dark
then set out. 'His heart was elated
over the bleak and dreary mountain
called Rimside Moor.'

4

below the ridge
above wind-inscribed stone
drop shadowed in moss

a buzzard splays
                    stilled wind
and lifts,
in the cold updraft
of the valley's steep incline,
a hung moment

dark clouds contour pale
a glow of veiled sun
in hail in hill fog
thickens mist with light

like my heart
a lark starts up
its striding song

long on pauses
flaffs a fast wind forward

sheep trails entwine the west face
a hare breaks
                as though, I thought

5

He retrieved the hidden pipes
and 'would never part with them again,
the gift of the Countess
and valued above riches.'

6

she sat astride me
in the dark
and we were drunk

rain on the attic roof
a random patterning of impact

or was it
static from her stockings
lit the room
an instrument
I was inside of

7

News of his escape came to Rothbury
and a bar-room army formed in his defence
but he knew it was hopeless
and could move faster alone.
A messenger was sent to Alnwick Castle
saying how ashamed he was of his ways
and the servants sent back a genteel suit,
four shirts, several pairs of stockings,
handkerchiefs and three guineas—which he
gambled and drank until a party
of five selected redcoats and their sergeant
approached the public house and gave chase.

He was at the summit of Rothbury crags
before they'd made the base
and couldn't resist saluting them
from a cairn stacked on the crag
and waited
till he could be sure of a hit
then stoned them from a-height.

The sergeant ordered his fleeing men to fire
but was struck on the shoulder with a rock
and gave a belated retreat.
'Vexed and alarmed they sullenly re-entered Rothbury.
It would be impossible to take him there
without surprise as almost every door was open
and every arm raised to defend him.'

a short-eared owl flew past
through mist-quick leaves of grass

NEWCASTLE COURANT

13TH AUGUST 1803

The tenants and other friends of the family were entertained by Earl Percy in the true style of old English hospitality, in the hall of the Castle,—and great plenty of ale was distributed to the populace, at the Castle's gates, and in the market place.—The Duke intends immediately to embody his corp. of tenantry, at his own expense, to the amount, we hear, of 1400 strong, who are to be instructed in the art of sharp shooting with rifle guns; and of which corps Earl Percy is to be Colonel.

JOIN THE ARMY

They said join the army and be a recruit—
they paid me five guineas, I bought a new suit.
They said join the army to be a recruit:
there's plenty of glory and arms full of loot.
The marching and drilling weren't worth the shilling,
but I let the gets think I was willing.
So I played them my pipes until late,
slipped the corporal one over eight;
the sergeant got drunk, the corpulent skunk,
in the morning he found I was doing a bunk.
I ran them through ditches and ran them up cloughs,
but those sons of bitches just hadn't the puff.
So I'm up and I'm running while they do their gunning,
I'm up and I'm running while they do their gunning.
I went on the run, it's a battle I won,
I was hot on the trot and I dodged their best shot.

A slash and a flash in my gentleman's suit—
cutting a dash as an army recruit!

They said join the army and be a recruit—
they paid me five guineas, I bought a new suit.

They said join the army to be a recruit:
there's plenty of glory and arms full of loot.
The marching and drilling weren't worth the shilling—
I can tell you I just wasn't willing.
I sent back the horse with a note,
saying thanks for the cash you old stoat.
I did it so often my name became known
in the Book of Deserters, a war office tome.
I rode through the night with the wind blowing fast,
the troopers gave chase but always came last.
So I'm up and I'm running while they do their gunning,
I'm up and I'm running while they do their gunning.
They took out their pistols and fired in the dark,
but I was away with the bright morning lark.

A slash and a flash in my gentleman's suit—
cutting a dash as an army recruit!

When I hid in the hills around Rothbury town
the people just gave them a right run around.
Have you seen him? they axed. Could you say he's about?
He's slippy as eels and flash as a trout.
We've looked on the fells and down in the dales
and all that we catch is a sight of his tail.
The people replied have you tried owa there?

He's sleek as a fox and runs like a hare.
There's no one can see him when he comes around,
the dogs go all quiet and cats go to ground.
But word got around that I was about—
an old flame betrayed me, the soldiers gave rout.
So I'm up and I'm running while they do their gunning,
I'm up and I'm running while they do their gunning.
I was lying in bed, they kicked in the door,
I tried to escape but was kicked to the floor.

A slash and a flash in my gentleman's suit—
cutting a dash as an army recruit!

WAR OFFICE

2ND NOVEMBER 1756

Sir

I am directed by the Secretary of War to return his thanks for your care of His Majesties Service in Committing to the County Gaol of Gloucester James Allan a Deserter from Col. Arabin's Reg. of Foot and to acquaint you that orders go by this night's post to fetch the Man away.

WAR OFFICE

22ND NOVEMBER 1757

Sir

I am directed by the Sec. at War to return you his thanks for your Care of His Maj. Service in Committing to York Gaol, James Allan a Deserter from M. S. Cornwallis's Reg. of Foot and to acquaint you that an Order goes by this Post to fetch the man away.

FETCH THE MAN AWAY

fetch the man away they say fetch the man away
fetch the man away they say fetch the man away

flech him back to camp and bind him to a wheel
paint the cobbles black when you whip him till he peels

fetch the man away they say fetch the man away
flech the man all day they say fetch the man away

flay him till he stays they say flech the man all day
flay him till he stays they say fetch the man away

fetch him to his regiment tie him to a wheel
bend him break him rip his skin whip him till he squeals

flay him till he stays fella fetch the man away
flay him till he stays fella flech the man all day

DURHAM LOCKUP: DESERTER

13TH NOVEMBER 1810

I left Annie and took up with Nell Clark.
She could do anything—tell fortunes, mend pots,
make pin cushions, and had the fastest hands
and was the boldest thief I've ever met.
She had more fingers than a bishop
and more faces than a duke.

NELL CLARK

Jamie move on
it's time to leave town
Jamie pack your pipes
and pass me my gown
he caught me up a back street
took me on the take
stalking in the shadows
he watched me like a snake
when I stepped out on the highway
to see what lay in sight
he was close behind me
like the shadow of a knife
when I had his fortune
lying in my palm
he closed his eyes
between my thighs
when they opened
I was gone
Jamie move on
it's time to leave town

Jamie pack your pipes and pass me my gown
I hollowed out his wallet
but I never took the bullet
from his gun
Jamie move on it's time to leave town
Jamie pack your pipes and pass me my gown
Jamie move on pack your pipes and run

dragged me up an alley
called me his gypsy child
in the creature darkness
I was quick and mild
if I would be an angel
when his friends came into town
I could lie in sleekest silk
or a shroud of eiderdown
I could spin fortunes
for a gentleman like him
with my dark gypsy eyes
and soft gypsy skin
if I would be his
as fortune foretold
string my hair with silver
lace his tongue with gold
he could 'prove my prospects

as justice of the peace
my life strung before him
tugging on a lease

Jamie move on it's time to leave town
Jamie pack your pipes and pass me my gown
I hollowed out his wallet
but I never took the bullet
from his gun

he said I will take you
to a house that lies near
I followed him closely
he called me his dear
I slipped him a drink
that sent him to sleep
when he wakes in the morning
he'll find I'm not cheap
when he wakes in the morning
his purse will be gone
his silk shirt and waistcoats
come on try them on
let's pack up and go
the sun's about due
pack up your pipes

he knows about you
Jamie come on
it's just a small risk
you can't live for ever
and the gallows are quick

I hollowed out his wallet
but I never took the bullet
from his gun

DURHAM LOCKUP

13TH NOVEMBER 1810

The wind's a prowling wolf
making forays—
A quick sniff, a curled lip, then it's gone.
And back.

Nell cut too close to the crop
and wore the shadow of the noose
for a necklace.

And kept dangerous company.

THOMAS RIDLEY,
HIS INFORMATION

14TH MARCH 1787

1

Robson locked the outer door of Craw Crag
and went to bed, while Elizabeth
and their three-year-old child went to another.
At about eleven there was a knock
and Robson shouted what do you want?
'We've missed the road to Sewing Shiel,
will you show us the way?'
But he wouldn't.

Andy Gordon and John Young were 'tall,
swarthy and ill-coloured' and Andy Allan,
'a little man,' kept watch in the yard.

Gordon found some iron harrow teeth
and began forcing and shifting the hinges
until the door was loose enough to kick in.
They grabbed and punched the couple

and threatened to kill them
if they wouldn't turn out the money.
John said we'll not leave without it
and started to search but could find none.

They took clothing belonging to Robson and Elizabeth
and to their nephew Thomas Ridley.
A black coat and waistcoat,
a black cloth cloak,
a black cape gown, a black silk hood,
a blue apron,
a pair of black leather men's gloves,
a pair of black leather women's gloves,
a strait coat and waistcoat,
a white gauze hood,
two white silk handkerchiefs,
two white linen handkerchiefs,
a pair of linen sheets,
a pair of brown cloth breeches with a patch between the legs,
two pairs of worsted stockings
and a man's hat with a crape band.

When he had the gear out Young turned and said
if you make a noise or start a hue and cry
we'll come back and kill you.

2

Thomas Ridley was informed that some 'night hawks'
were going towards Cumberland and gave chase.
By the time he reached Haltwhistle
they had been cuffed and carted to Carlisle Gaol
where he saw John Young and
'challenged the hat upon his head'
and the pair of brown cloth breeches
keeping his arse warm.

3

Jane Allan and Margaret Young were seen with pack asses
leaving Carlisle.
Ridley followed with the High Constable, Robert Raven,
and at midnight found the two women camped on Goathill.
Their bags were searched and some of Ridley's clothing found
and that of his aunt and uncle Robson.
The women denied theft but said some prisoners gie us.

JOHN CLARK, HIS INFORMATION

3RD FEBRUARY 1788

1

Do you want to mek enough to buy yourself some shoes?
John Winter asked John Clark.
And with his son Robert and a Scot called Drummond
went to the house of William and Hannah Hog
—both eighty-six years old and in bed with the door bolted.

At about eight o'clock, while Clark kept watch
the others used a three-pronged iron grape
to force the door. When it burst open
Hannah recognised the men, having bought,
the week before, horn spoons from Peg Winter.

Robert held Hog by the throat
while John beat his head with the grape—
leaving severe cuts over his right eye and left arm.

Hannah was dragged to her knees and slapped
damn thee thou's money for the cow just selt.
But they never had a cow.
John said turn out the money or I'll kill thee.

When Clark heard the scream he came in
and pulled John away by the coat
who snarled—thou'll get the same for that!
There's money in the hoos, man.

They took fourteen linen shirts, eighteen linen caps,
three white linen handkerchiefs, one black silk hood,
three good linen sheets, one bed gown,
a woollen coat, a waistcoat and breeches,
three cakes of bread and some butter.

Before leaving they broke the bedstead
and everything they possibly could.

2

They then went by Rede Bridge
and were taking three horses from a stable
when a dog barked and Drummond panicked
and let his horse go.
Robert haltered one and bridled another
and they rode double to Bellingham
to screw a carpenter's shop
for some chisels and a spiked gimlet.

They forded the North Tyne well after midnight
and left the horses tied to a tree
while they walked through the snow
to the mansion house at Hesleyside.
When they came to a gate
about thirty yards from the house,
John Winter told Clark
stay here, and whistle if anybody shows.

Robert smashed a window and climbed in,
followed by his father and Drummond.

They brought back two large bundles
wrapped in worn woollen blankets
which they tied together by the corners
and slung across a horse.
The bundles contained a silver-plated quart tankard,
two white linen counterpane quilts,
one printed cotton quilt, four linen napkins,
one damask table cloth,
three linen breakfast table cloths,
two very fine woollen blankets,
one double woollen blanket,
one black silk bonnet,
one black silk cap called a Robin Grey,
two linen pillow slips, one coarse linen sheet,
one red leather pocket book lined with blue silk,
one green silk purse.

They re-crossed the river, hid the bundles in a stone quarry
and made Swindon by noon, where they met
Peg Winter and her daughters Phyllis and Jane.

3

Next morning at seven John Winter said to John Clark
let's gan and get the money for your shoes.

And just before noon, outside the village of Holystone,
Robert took a tankard from his coat
and gave it to his mother, Peg, who put it under her clothes.
They went into the alehouse and John ordered drinks for them all.

When Purvis asked for payment John Winter said I'll gie it
when the money comes for a horse I selt.
And how about a loan to get young Clark shod?

Purvis only had two shilling but Winter told him
I'm sure you'll find more when you see this
and offered 'a silver tankard for only ten guineas.'

Purvis said it's plated, the copper's coming through.
Thee, said John Winter giving it to Clark,

thine eyesight is better. But he wasn't a judge of silver
and gave it back.

Well, what will you give? Winter asked Purvis.
No more than two shillings.
And Peg sold him three linen shirts for six.

4

At daybreak Clark, Robert Winter and Drummond
returned to the quarry with an ass to collect their swag.
About a mile from Elsdon they found a line of clothes
stretched across a garden and took them.
And at midnight screwed two cotton gowns from
a house at the north end of the village.

Before dawn they joined the rest of the Winter family
hiding out at John Robinson's farm at High Farnham
and stashed some of the gear there.
The rest was spread between James Ord's farm at Shaperton
'as he frequently harbours vagrants of every denomination'
and a watchmaker's in Rothbury.

Clark asked John Winter for his shoe money
And was told 'I've got nowt
and that's what you'll get.' Clark said
you'd better give me sumit or al 'peach you.
And John Winter said you'll not do much talking
with your throat ripped out.

JOHN CLARK, HIS INFORMATION

NOVEMBER 1787

1

You can have that twenty I owe
if you come with me and Walter
to screw Wilkie's grainary at Doddington,
Hugh Stewart told John Clark over a drink at Holystone.

There's a lock on the grainary impossible to pick:
I tried it but I could not pick it, Walter said.
But I got some cheese out the window.

We will get the lock picked, no fear,
Hugh Steward said, and turned to Jane Purvis.
You'll be ready Thursday morning?

And what shall I have for this trouble?
At least a stone of wool, I hope?

Both Hugh and Walter assured her,
you'll not want for cheeses neither.

What time in the morning?
About four, Stewart thought.
It's market day, I'll get rid of them quick,
she reckoned.

John, Walter and Hugh agreed to meet next day
at the Bell and Dean,
half a mile from Tweedmouth
—late afternoon.

2

Hugh brought a Galloway and Walter two asses
to carry what they could get from Wilkie's grainary.
They arrived about ten at night and left the animals
a safe distance, at the Black Barn.
Hugh told John to watch Wilkie's house
in case anyone came out.
He was there two hours before they came back,
carrying a sack of wool each and complaining it was hard
to break open the under-lock.
After loading the wool onto the Galloway
they went back to the grainary
and tied three sacks of cheeses onto the asses
and travelled together as far as the Bell and Dean
where, at four a.m., they gave John a sack to take home.

Later that morning he met Hugh and Walter at the Purvis alehouse.
Hugh's wife put some wool onto a sheet, tied the four corners
and gave it to Walter's wife, Isabel Donovan, alias Moss,
who went out and was back within an hour with it sold.
The money went into Jane's pocket.

She turned to Hugh and said you did a good job,
shearing the wool from that humpback, Wilkie.
He can well afford it.

They were still drinking when handbills were posted.
She told them you'd better had away quick
if you don't want taking. They won't suspect John,
so he can gan yem to his wife and bairns.

ROBERT LOWRY, HIS INFORMATION

2ND–5TH MARCH 1788

Two 'wandering men,' John and Robert Winter,
forced the lock on Lowry's stable
and stole a white-faced, dun-bellied bay mare with a switch tail
and a white scratch down her face
and rode it north.

Two days later, at Badochside near Moffat,
they asked John Marchbank for a doss
and offered to swop the bay mare for his grey mare
and five shillings. Marchbank only had two on him
but would owe the rest.

On discovering the theft
Lowry followed the footmarks north
but lost the trail.
A week later he was informed
that Marchbank had his mare
and rode into Scotland to retrieve it.

Marchbank said he might have such a horse
but refused to part with it without proof of ownership.
And a guinea for stabling.
Lowry rode back to Northumberland for his brother
and Robert Bell,
a blacksmith who'd shod the horse.

Meanwhile Marchbank raised an armed posse
and found the tinklers dossing in a barn
where he showed them a warrant. Robert Winter ran
and was caught and offered a silver watch to let him go.

WALTER SCOTT, HIS INFORMATION

ABBOTSFORD, MELROSE, 25TH APRIL 1818

I knew something of Allan's Grandfather or perhaps Great Grandfather. They were Yetholmers & retainers at one time of the Marquesses of Lothian ... Living near to Fairnihurst, the castle of the Marquesses of Lothian three miles above Jedburgh was a certain Bold yeoman called Rengan Oliver, one of the strongest men in our Country. This man was much irritated by the Marquess repeatedly hunting over his fields when the corn was growing & at length to mark his resentment of the injury he shot one of the Dogs. The Marquess in revenge came to his house at Smailcleugh with a party, and among the rest Allan, all of them boys of the belt who were to do the Lairds bidding right or wrong. Rengan had secured his doors and windows with withies fastened across them and fired out on the assailants while a Maid servant the only other person within the house loaded his guns of which he had two or three. He made good his defence till a shot killed the poor maid on which Rengan cut down the withies and rushed desperately out on his assailants with an axe in one hand and his Broadsword in the other. His foot however being entangled on the withy he stumbled and ere he could recover himself Allan the tinker struck him down with a Mell or hammer. Rengan was made prisoner and sent to Edinburgh where he died. But his son was 'upsides' with Allan to whom he gave a most dreadful beating at the pass above Inchbonny near Jedburgh.

When I first saw James Allan at the Kelso races he wore the Northumberland livery, a Blue coat with a silver crescent on his arm. He was an admirable piper but a desperate reprobate. The last time I saw him he was in absolute beggary and had behaved so ill at my uncle's house that the old Gentleman himself most admirable piper would not give him Quarters though I interceded earnestly for him 'the Knave' as Davie tells Justice Shallow 'being my very good friend.' He was then quite like a Pauper with his wife and an ass in true Gypsy fashion.

A LOW SKY

A low sky hung on the hills, hunched and harried
like their shoulders—and the ragged Gallowa.

The weather was like the border,
ill-definable, and sometimes impenetrable.

They found a clough deep in rock
below a wind that screamed a sack of cats.

They'd been there before and they'd be there again.
If the storm hadn't ripped they'd of made Kelso by dusk.

But anywhere is where they were going,
and there was as good as it got.

Annie found a windbreak and gathered kindling,
quickly, without talking.

They ate in silence, and when they finished lay close,
listening to the wind and the fire's crack.

THE RIVER IS DARK

The river is dark with peat from the fell,
curlews are calling with nothing to tell.
Leave my house and leave my home,
Jamie pack your bags and roam—
and like the fox you shall grieve.

The waters of Scotland so wild and sleek,
take them now and take them deep.
Never return to your own running Tyne
as long as the river's a river of mine.

Live by the Teviot, die by it too,
while I wait by the Tyne but not waiting for you.
The border is long and the border is wide
with many a water and many a bride
for you to love and live beside
and drown in the running tide—
and like the fox you shall grieve.

Goodbye to the river, goodbye to the fell,
goodbye to the days too loving to tell.

Goodbye to the drink, goodbye to the craic,
goodbye to the nights with you on my back.

The river is black with peat from the fell,
curlews are calling with nothing to tell.
Leave me now and let me sleep,
your thieving words are all I'll keep—
and like the fox you shall grieve.

BALLAD OF PRECIPITATION

I thought roving over
and wandering passed

but now I am footloose
with my shoe on a last

the river beneath us
the sky flew ahead

you and I in a fast bed

but now I am footloose
with my shoe on the last

and a chaste sky chases
a river that's passed

HAWTHORN

there is a hawthorn on a hill
there is a hawthorn growing
it set its roots against the wind
the worrying wind that's blowing
its berries are red its blossom so white
I thought that it was snowing

there is a hawthorn by a wall
that looks down to the valley
its berries are red its thorns are sharp
it's where we said we'd marry
its berries are red its blossom is white
and the hail makes sharp weather
without her now I'll make my bed
in the bleeding heather

come with me oh come with me
come with me my darling
the berries are red the thorns are sharp
and the corbies are craawing
don't send me out don't cut me down
don't exile me my darling

the thorns turn red kill the blossom dead
and the tethered wind is snarling

there is a hawthorn by a wall
that looks down to the valley
its berries are red its thorns are sharp
it's where we said we'd marry
its berries are red its blossom is white
and the hail makes sharp weather
without her now I'll make my bed
in the bleeding heather

BALLAD OF JAMIE ALLAN

they said no jail could hold me
at the age of twenty-five
but now I am past seventy
and chained up to my lies
my wife and child are begging
for money in the street
while I lie in Durham jail
beneath a cold crime sheet

the wind sings Jamie Allan, oh

my daughter lives in Alnwick
like I did before
the music that she plays
her trade is sweet amore
she's living with a madam
a woman of lewd repute
ploughing for the court
that hang about the duke

I was horse thief to his majesty
for dukes and earls I ponced
and when I asked for mercy
a smile was their response
I was horse thief to his majesty
for earls and dukes I played
but I'm dying in a cell
that dukes and earls have made

I played my pipes for cut-throats
my hautboy for counts
I played for dukes and dykers
and beggars with the bunce
I played my tunes for soldier boys
bleeding on the line
I played my jigs for generals
their buckets of red wine

I was horse thief to his majesty
deserter to the king
I played my pipes for a countess
and made her poor heart sing
I was horse thief to his majesty
for dukes and earls I piped

but I'm lying in a cell
and dying in my shite

they said no jail could hold me
at the age of forty-four
when jailors' wives and daughters
opened up the doors
but now that I am old and frail
and cannot pick the lock
I must die in Durham jail
but will not be forgot

the wind sings Jamie Allan, oh

DURHAM LOCKUP

13TH NOVEMBER 1810

so go and play your pipes
and wing your violin
the wind is howling through the dyke
but you will not let me in

the reeds that grow
through dunes of snow
play an icy pitch
but while I've breath
I'll warm them, 'less
death turns out the broom

when death turns out the broom
we'll all be swept, with nothing
but blossoms on the broom

then who will play my pipes
or you your violin
when the wind is howling through the dyke
and the dancers within

NEWCASTLE COURANT

17TH NOVEMBER 1810

On Tuesday last, in the house of correction at Durham, where he had been confined upwards of seven years, under sentence of transportation for life, James Allan a character well known in most parts of the united kingdom, but particularly in Northumberland. He went by the name of Jemmy the Duke's piper, and was in his early life a great proficient on the pipes. He was capitally convicted of horse stealing at the assizes at Durham in 1803, and received sentence of death, but was afterwards pardoned on condition of transportation for life; but on account of his age and infirmities, his conduct could not be carried into execution. He had nearly completed his 76th year, and for the greater part of his confinement was afflicted with a complication of diseases.

clouds drag shadows across contours
storms hail between hassock
while west winds chase light
chasing vapour from the coast

a raven blows in with a croak
and settles on a cairn
hears grass respond to gusts

pale golden reeds are black
reflected in a pool
whose surface stippled wind
as her dress fell, light
as a shadow on her body

and if she were next to me now
all night under the low beams
and shifting tiles
beneath the wind
held for a moment

as it passes and is forgotten
like a dream on waking
or a blown note
honed to silence

Afterword

What business hath he to keep Company with Lords and
Gentlemen? he should leave them to prey upon one another.

JOHN GAY, *The Beggar's Opera*

I became a dealer of sorts in my mid-teens and used to hang around
the auction rooms in Newcastle's Gallowgate where the contents of
houses were sold. The owners had died off and their relatives, if
there were any, had arranged for the houses to be cleared. Some of
the items weren't worth enumerating and were sold unlisted by the
tea-chestful in a former stable, across the yard from the main auc-
tion room. One day, in such a box, I found a broken-backed but
complete copy of the book

Life of James Allan,
the celebrated Northumbrian piper;
containing his surprising adventures
and wonderful achievements in England, Scotland,
Ireland, France, India, Tartary, Russia,
Egypt, and various other Countries of Europe,
Asia, and Africa.

Taken principally from his own relation.

The author is Andrew Wight and this second edition was issued in
1818 by the radical Newcastle publisher, MacKenzie. The picaresque

book is 672 pages long. Two other biographies of Jamie Allan were published within a few years of each other. They were followed over a hundred years by chapbooks and pamphlets that were sold throughout the Borders where his name and exploits entertained the peoples of the region.

More contemporary people will hear his name, at least, when they first take up the pipes or fiddle and learn a tune called 'Jimmy Allan,' and might wonder sometimes who he was. And perhaps those fictitious musicians who played that tune as the ship went down in the Hollywood movie, *Titanic*, might also have wondered who he was. Hollywood is not so far-fetched from the story: a lot of Harry Potter was shot in Alnwick Castle, home of the dukes of Northumberland. The archives of Alnwick Castle are bereft of any mention of Allan, I am assured (not having the wherewithal to peruse those dusty catacombs myself). However, he stubbornly sticks to the location in his erroneous sometimes appellation of 'Jemmy, the Duke's piper.'

So who was James Allan? There is the memory of him sketched by Walter Scott in a letter to a bookseller when ordering a copy of the biography in 1817, and there is the image created by the book that he was ordering (so niftily illustrated by Robert Cruikshank). Both are true, but one truth was made out of the other; legends are subject, by their nature, to embellishment. And there is an official document here and there. He left nothing tangible behind him, beyond the human gift of his genes. There is no question that he was a magnificent musician, and it is also unquestionable, I would assert—

given his nature and need—that he improvised continually. Perhaps those tunes, airs upon air, his inventions, might be passed along still.

He was an almost exact contemporary of George III. But whereas George inherited and left social structures and edifices in place, what has Jamie Allan left for us to know him by? Some social historians are aware of him. His only appearance in *Rogues, Thieves and the Rule of Law* by Gwenda Morgan and Peter Rushton—a scholarly look at criminal life on this side of the Scottish Border in the eighteenth century—is in the first paragraph:

> The North-East appeared remote and alien to people from the rest of England. For one thing, in the eighteenth century the region had only recently emerged from the Border lawlessness which had characterised it for centuries. Some picaresque accounts of eighteenth-century characters such as the famous piper James Allan suggest that this image remained both powerful and attractive. His wandering, musically creative, intermittently criminal, life was dramatized after his death in 1810 (in Durham gaol) by accounts which stressed the casual subculture of the marginal economy of the Borders, with a pattern of individual employment drifting in and out of crime. If even half the story is true, Allan was remarkably lucky to have respectable patrons who rescued him from transportation or even the gallows.

'Besides, Certainty gives a Man a good Air upon his Tryal, and makes him risque another without Fear or Scruple,' as Filch says to Mrs Peachum. And the great Huddie Ledbetter—who sang, 'when

91

your shoes wear out, you're back on your feet again'—was twice given official pardons after singing for the governor of the state in which he was incarcerated. I suspect like many itinerant musicians, he spent his life travelling from one empty belly to the next.

A number of the poems here were written from the sworn depositions and 'informations' of Allan's known associates and their accusers stored in the criminal records of the National Archives. Other poems are informed by his military—he features regularly in the Book of Deserters—and criminal records. It was a thrill to blow a layer of two-hundred-year-old dust off the scroll of old documents from his last trial of 1803. Here was proof of the man—and as it turned out with another earlier information, proof of his brother Robert, also a piper, fellow horse thief and professional deserter. Jamie also claimed that he broke his brother out of Edinburgh Castle where he was being held as a deserter. Although the crimes of his occasional 'known associates,' the Winters and the Clarks, were often brutal, Jamie only ever once took part in a violent robbery—in London—and he felt great remorse for it. As a criminal his *modus operandi* was cunning and an inventive trickery that often enabled him to outfox his pursuers and captors.

In 1791, Nell Clark, his one-time partner, was convicted for murder and hung with her fellow murderess, Jane Clark. William Winter was hung with them for the same crime and then gibbeted for the crows to consume. The two women were publicly anatomized where it was discovered, 'notwithstanding the apparent looseness of the life they led,' one of them had her hymen intact. As Michel Foucault writes, 'Justice pursues the body beyond all possible pain.'

One notable nineteenth-century local historian, referring to Jamie Allan, said 'his history would be better left unwritten,' yet his story has clung on stubbornly in the collective Border memory, not just because he was a clever rogue, but because he was a musician of genius. When he couldn't live by his pipes he stole horses, or joined the army for the recruiting money and deserted the same day. I doubt if he saw anything incompatible in the two lifestyles. His crimes were for survival not accumulation. The after-effects of those crimes died with the criminal, whereas those of his contemporary betters, those who enclosed common ground, remain with us and shape the landscape.

Allan was not alone in running afoul of recruitment practices. Ralph Soulsby Esq., the same justice of the peace to whom Jamie was brought when captured in Hexham as a deserter, was also officiating six months later, during the Hexham Militia Riot on 9th March 1761. On that occasion, one soldier and at least fifty demonstrators were killed during an anti-recruiting demonstration estimated to number five thousand.

My nod to *The Beggar's Opera* is not so fanciful, either; Allan's father, Will, himself a notable piper, named one of his favourite dogs Peachum. And it was his father, it is alleged, when once asked if he wasn't going to help rescue his son from the threat of the gallows said, 'Many a better man has felt the weight of his arse.' However, when Hanoverian soldiers surrounded the house, he did run away disguised as Jamie while his mother shouted 'run Jamie, run,' giving their son, the deserter, time to escape.

The place where Allan died, under the Old Elvet Bridge over the river Wear in Durham City, was the last extant 'lock up' in the North before being turned into a nightclub cellar bar called the *Jimmy Allan*. It is dark and dank to this day. Cruel fate for an old musician with the fells in his soul whose wish was to be buried back in the laws of his birthplace in the Upper Coquet Valley. Before any of his friends knew of it his body was disposed of in a pauper's grave at St Nicholas's Parish, Durham, which has long since been demolished leaving no marker. From his incarceration in 1803 to his death in 1810 Annie travelled all over the Borders with their son raising what nourishment she could for Jamie, keeping his name alive as she did so.

A small token of sorts: the folk opera of *Ballad of Jamie Allan* which John Harle and I wrote, and in which Kathryn Tickell played the Northumbrian pipes, was commissioned by The Sage Gateshead and performed there, co-incidentally, a few paces from the scene of his last crime where he stole Matthew Robinson's bay mare. And we afterwards discovered that the premier fell, fortuitously, on Jamie Allan's birthday. The songs and some of the narrative in this book form the basis of the opera.

Selected Resources

BOOKS & ESSAYS

Askew, Gilbert. 'The Origins of the Northumbrian Pipes.' *Archaeologia Aeliana*, 4th ser., 9 (1932): 63–83.

Buchan, David. *The Ballad and the Folk.* London: Routledge & Kegan Paul, 1972.

Cashman, Ray. 'The Heroic Outlaw in Irish Folklore and Popular Literature.' *Folklore* 111, no. 2 (Oct., 2000): 191–215.

Child, Francis James, ed. *The English and Scottish Popular Ballads.* 5 vols. Boston and New York: Houghton, Mifflin & Co., 1882–98.

Corfe, Tom. *Riot: The Hexham Militia Riot, 1761.* Hexham: Hexham Community Partnership, 2004.

Cowper, R. A. S. 'The Ducal Pipers at Alnwick Castle, Northumberland.' *Archaeologia Aeliana*, 4th ser., 41 (1963): 195–204.

Foucault, Michel. *Discipline and Punish: The Birth of the Prison.* Trans. Alan Sheridan. Rev. ed. London: Penguin, 1991.

Gay, John. *The Beggar's Opera and Polly: together with the airs of the music from the original editions of 1728 and 1729.* London: Chapman & Dodd, 1923.

Grigson, Geoffrey, ed. *The Penguin Book of Ballads.* Harmondsworth: Penguin, 1975.

Harker, Dave. *Fakesong: The Manufacture of British 'Folksong' 1700 to the Present Day.* Milton Keynes: Open University Press, 1985.

———. 'The Making of the Tyneside Concert Hall.' *Popular Music* 1 (1981): 27–30. Harker looks at Allan as an illustration of musicians moving from a rural to an industrial audience in the eighteenth century.

Hobsbawm, Eric. *Bandits*. London: Weidenfeld & Nicolson, 2000.

Lemire, Beverly. 'Peddling Fashion: Salesmen, Pawnbrokers, Taylors, Thieves and the Second-Hand Clothes Trade in England, c. 1700–1800.' *Textile History* 22 (1991): 67–82.

———. 'The Theft of Clothes and Popular Consumerism in Early Modern England.' *Journal of Social History* 24, no. 2. (Winter, 1990): 255–76.

Lloyd, A. L. *Folk Song in England*. London: Lawrence & Wishart, 1967.

Morgan, Gwenda and Peter Rushton. *Rogues, Thieves and the Rule of Law: The Problem of Law Enforcement in North-East England, 1718–1800*. London: UCL Press, 1998.

Paredes, Américo. *'With His Pistol in His Hand': A Border Ballad and Its Hero*. Austin: University of Texas Press, 1958.

Reed, James, ed. *The Border Ballads*. London: Athlone Press, 1973.

Spraggs, Gillian. *Outlaws & Highwaymen: The Cult of the Robber in England from the Middle Ages to the Nineteenth Century*. London: Pimlico, 2001.

Styles, John. 'Print and Policing: Crime Advertising in Eighteenth-Century Provincial England.' In *Policing and Prosecution in Britain, 1750–1850*, ed. Douglas Hay and Francis Snyder, 55–97. Oxford: Clarendon Press, 1989.

Swinburne, Algernon Charles. *Ballads of The English Border*. Ed. William A. MacInnes. London: William Heinemann, 1925.

Sykes, John. *Local Records; or Historical Register of Remarkable Events, which Have Occurred in Northumberland and Durham, Newcastle Upon Tyne, and Berwick Upon Tweed, from the Earliest Period of Authentic Record, to the Pre-*

sent Time; with Biographical Notices of Deceased Persons of Talent, Eccentricity, and Longevity. 2 vols. Newcastle upon Tyne, 1833.

Thompson, E. P. *The Making of The English Working Class.* Rev. ed. London: Penguin, 1991.

Thompson, James. *A New Improved, and Authentic Life of James Allan, The Celebrated Northumberland Piper; detailing his surprising adventures in Various Parts of Europe, Asia, and Africa. Including a complete description of the Manners and Customs of the Gypsy Tribe. Collected from sources of genuine authority.* With explanatory notes by E. Mackenzie. Newcastle upon Tyne, 1828.

Wight, Andrew. *Life of James Allan, the celebrated Northumbrian piper; containing his surprising adventures and wonderful achievements in England, Scotland, Ireland, France, India, Tartary, Russia, Egypt, and various other Countries of Europe, Asia, and Africa. Taken principally from his own relation.* 2nd ed. Newcastle upon Tyne: Mackenzie & Dent, 1818.

WEBSITES

To hear what the Northumbrian pipes sound like you could do no better than listen to my friend Kathryn Tickell (no mean fiddler, either): www.kathryntickell.com.

Matt Seattle, an excellent musician, has useful links on his site and information on the instruments: www.dragonflymusic.co.uk. He also republishes books of the old pipe tunes.

For a history of highwaymen and their predecessors, medieval outlaws, see: www.outlawsandhighwaymen.com.

Acknowledgements

In researching the life of James Allan, I consulted the following archives: the Newcastle Central Library, local collection, for eighteenth-century newspapers; the National Archives, Kew, for criminal depositions, case papers, indictments, and desertion records (ASSI 45/5/2/10–11, 45/33/1/1a–c; DURH 17/43; WP 4/594–596). The Scott letter is from *The Letters of Sir Walter Scott*, ed. H. J. C. Grierson (London: Constable & Co., Ltd., 1933), 4: 220–21.

John Harle has issued a studio recording of *Ballad of Jamie Allan* [Harle CD006] with the original performers: Omar Ebrahim, Balladeer; Sarah Jane Morris, Balladeer; Kathryn Tickell, Northumbrian Piper; Bill Patterson, Narrator; The Northern Sinfonia with Neil MacColl (guitar) and Steve Lodder (keyboards). It was released by www.harlerecords.com and distributed by www.selectmusic.co.uk. The opera is available for performance with permission from Chester music: www.chesternovello.com. We called *Ballad of Jamie Allan* a 'folk-opera,' although that label may be too 'classical' for the folk world and too 'folky' for the classical world. But like the subject of the story, it strides the borders where I'm always happy to pitch a tent.

A number of musician friends have engaged with me at various stages of this ongoing project and I would like to thank them: Peter Kirtley and Liane Carroll who recorded 'Away Boys Away'; Paul McCartney who gave the use of his studio and engineers for the occasion and who introduced me to John Harle; Ben Murray was a steadying friend during the writing and reeling of 'Hawthorn' and recorded a version of his own with Rosie Doonan—along with 'Dreaming Annie'—on *Mill Lane* [Silvertop CD001]; Kaythryn Tickell wrote the tune 'Hawthorn' with Corrina Hewat—'inspired' by my ballad of that name—available on *The Sky Didn't Fall* [Park CD88]. I rambled on a lot to Annie Lennox who listened patiently and recalled for me some of the Border Ballads that lived in her memory—commenting, 'to die for, literally.'

I am grateful to the late Raphael Samuels who tried, during tutorials in the back of taxies, to show me how to look at history. I would like to thank friends and colleagues who have opened the wicket gate and pointed to the delectable mountains: Bruce Jackson, Gwenda Morgan, Peter Rushton and William Lancaster.

Thanks also to: The Sage Gateshead and Folkworks which commissioned the opera, and Simon Clugston who directed it; the editors of *Square One* and *Chicago Review*, where some of this work was first published; Bill Corbett who published the song 'Ballad of Jamie Allan' as a broadside; Nicholas Johnson of Etruscan Press, for publishing an earlier version of 'Away Boys Away' as 'The Ballad of Jamie Allan' in *Fuckwind*; Chris Sutcliffe for filming so deftly the premier of the opera at extremely short notice; Newcastle University for access to the Robinson Library for a couple of years; Bob Aitken for some research assistance; Ian Henderson for keeping the car on the road; Bill Griffiths who helped me nail a word; Svava Barker for an earlier skirmish with Jamie. Other friends have been invaluable in their ways: Judith Ann Murphy; Tasha Lay; Anne Moore at Morpeth Chantry & Bagpipe Museum; Lindsay Levy at the Advocates Library, Parliament House, Edinburgh; my agents Tracey Elliston and Caroline Clayton at Judy Daish Associates Ltd.; and finally thanks to Devin Johnston and Michael O'Leary of Flood Editions for giving me a second bite at the cherry.

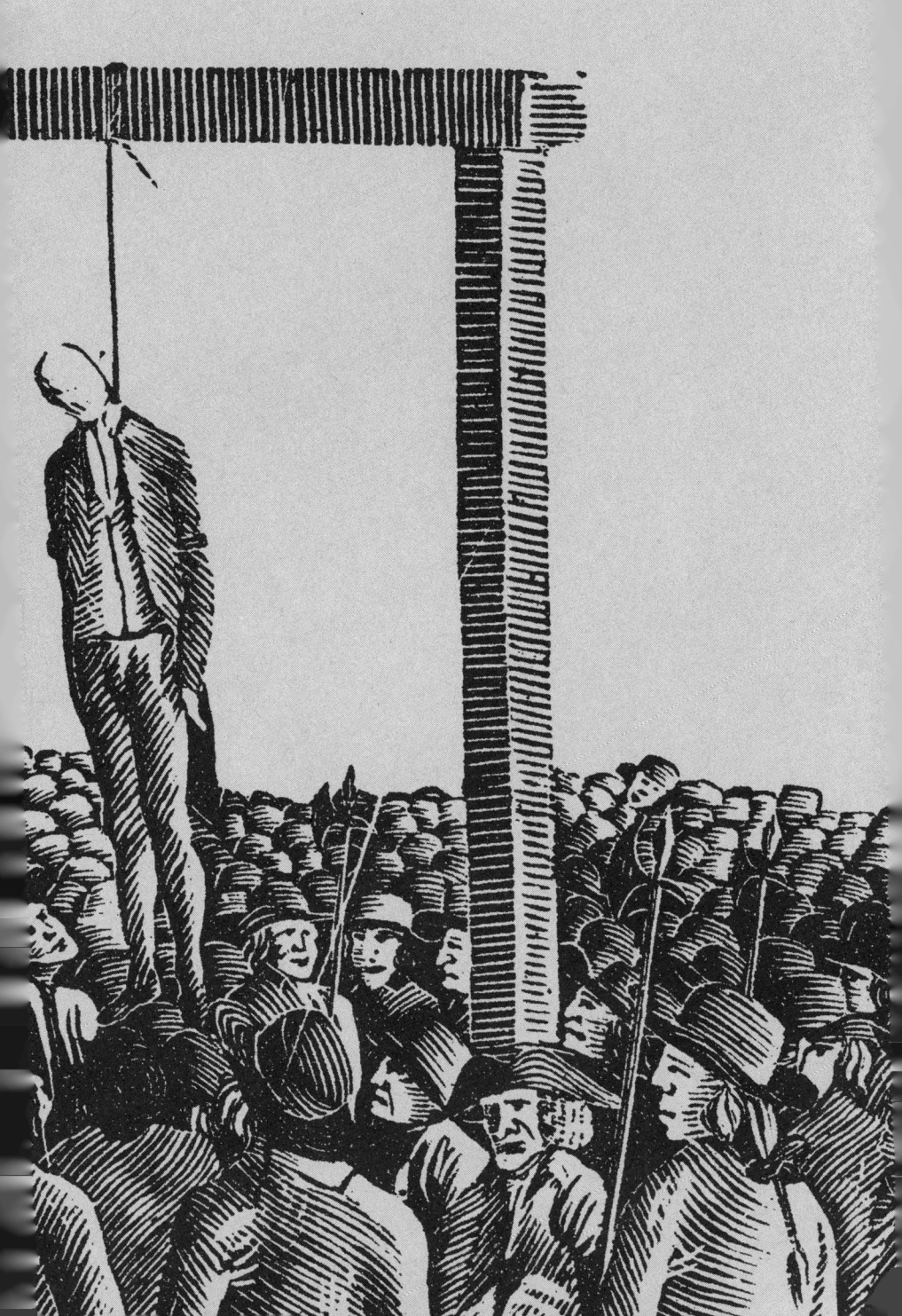

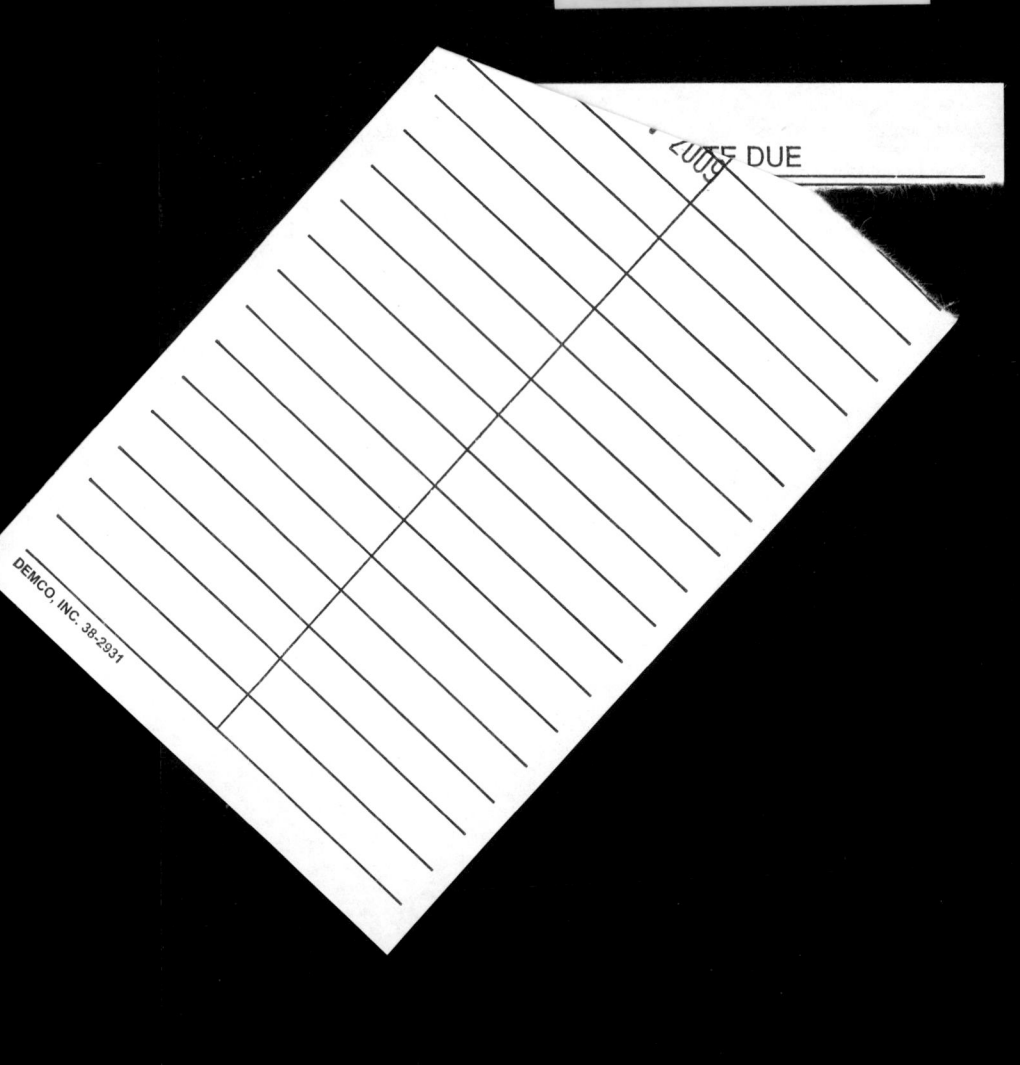